Mexican Slang

plus Graffiti

M. F. Jones-Reid
Charlene Lopez
L. H. Robinson

MEXICAN SLANG PLUS GRAFFITI

a *Bueno* Book

second edition, second printing, 2000
printing history:
second edition, revised and expanded, 1999 ISBN 1-881791-10-6
fourth printing, 1998
third printing, 1996
second printing, 1994
first edition, 1992 ISBN 0-9627080-7-0

Bueno Books, a division of
In One EAR Publications
PO Box 847
Round Rock TX 78680-0847

ISBN 1-881791-10-6

Library of Congress Cataloging in Publication Data

Jones-Reid, M. F. 1921-1995
Charlene Lopez 1943-1998
L. H. Robinson 1948-
Mexican slang plus graffiti / by M.F. Jones-Reid, Charlene Lopez and
L.H. Robinson. —2nd ed. p. cm.
Spanish phrases with English translation.
1. Spanish language—Slang. 2. Spanish language—Graffiti. I. Title.

Printed in the U.S.A.

Table of Contents

Sleazy Moral Disclaimer

You will notice right away that this lexicon contains a wide range of slang terms, including the vulgar and obscene. This was the result of a decision we made only after much soul-searching, moral discussion, and sniggering. We decided it would be pointless to omit phrases that are commonly heard. We are not advocating that readers run around foreign countries spewing nasty words, (and of course if you are offended by coarse language, read no further and all that) but it is helpful to know what is meant by words that one hears—and to know what words to avoid repeating.

To that end we have tried to categorize questionable words by the kind of company in which they are acceptable. "Polite" means acceptable in any company, "acceptable" means in mixed company of sophisticated adults. Carlos Colegiano and Omar Onda are the representatives who give examples for these slang expressions.

Aside from terms here that may be vulgar, crude, or downright nasty, there are others which, while acceptable, may have street connotations that would sound like "gutter talk" in polite company. Beto Boca de Basura and Luis Angel Lambada are your guides to riskier phrases that may be offensive as well as colorful.

Youthful slang can make your speech sound hip to some or silly and juvenile to others. It is not a bad idea to follow the example of your company when using vulgar or street terms, and to ask someone privately when in doubt. Also consider the difference in your age with the ages of your audience; a young slang-speaker might be considered impudent by an older audience, while an older slang-speaker might be absurd to a younger audience. If you commit a *faux pas*, it never hurts to include in your apology a reminder that you are not a native speaker.

Keep in mind that words change meaning in different countries. To call a man *cabrón*, for instance, is common and relatively tame in Mexico, but in Cuba and some other countries means that you have cuckolded him, and is a grave insult capable of turning a friend into an enemy instantly. It is best to be careful of insults at first, even playful ones. In Brazil, by the way, *cabrón* means "handsome" or "foxy."

Cobarde: es aquel que tiene el valor de decir que tiene miedo.

A coward is the one who has the courage to say that he's afraid.

El que no tiene enemigos no tiene incentivos.
——La Paz.

He who has no enemies has no incentives.
——Peace

Las mujeres buenas van al cielo ...las malas a cualquier parte.

Good girls go to heaven ...the bad ones wherever they want.

Entre más conozco al hombre,
más quiero a mi perro.
Atentamente, Veterinario

The more I get to know men,
the more I like my dog.
Cordially, The Veterinary

Hombre precavido
vale por dos.
Mujer precavida
tiene dos.

Perro
meador a
buen árbol
se arrima.

La pereza es la madre de todos los
vicios ... pero madre es madre y
hay que respetarla.
Atentamente, su Madre

Idleness is the mother of all vices
... but mothers are mothers and
must be respected.
(signed) your Mother.

Pared y muralla
para graffitiar cuando
den papaya.

The Obligatory Boring Scholarly Introduction

It would be impossible to discuss Spanish slang in totality, since there is different slang in every country and region. Mexico alone has a rich and multi-leveled idiomatic vocabulary of thousands of words, and many terms that are used colloquially in Chiapas are never heard in Veracruz. Furthermore, there are Dantesque levels of societal usage, some obscure or unknown even to Mexicans. However, our concern here is not esoteric folklore, but standard Mexican slang, words that are widely heard or read in comic books, TV shows, and rock music.

Within the wide and varied tapestry of Mexican slang are several main strains worth mention, specific examples of which are included later in the text:

La onda came out of 1960's hippie cant, but is still current and *¿Qué onda?* is a very common greeting among the young and hip. *Onda* means wave (as in microwave) or vibrations. *Buena onda* means, essentially "good vibes." *Ondas* are expressions, folkways, or manners. "YouthSpeak" would be *Ondas Adolescentes*; Mexican jokes and slang such as those in the this book would be *ondas mexicanas*. Carlos Colegiano is your mentor for chic phrases which are modern and hip, but not offensive. His buddy, Omar Onda, uses much of the same language, but is racier and pushes the limits of courtesy in mixed company.

Caló (a word which originally referred to the cant of Spanish gypsies) or *calichi* is underground, criminal argot, particularly from the poor barrios of Mexico City—pure gutter talk. As impenetrable as the similar Cockney slang, *caló* mutates as fast as ghetto rap or surfer lingo and there is always some new twist for the explorer. Luis Angel Lambada and Beto Boca de Basura will guide you through the tortuous and mysterious jungle of street talk and rude expressions. Their girlfriends help out from time to time.

"Spanglish" border talk, is also called *fronterazos* or *pochismos* after *pochos*, or Mexicans who live on the U.S. side of the border. Viewed by the academy as a degeneration of Spanish if not a form of linguistic imperialism, border usage is mercurial and often very funny. There are several ways in which English and Spanish meld: A Spanish word like *educación* which technically means "upbringing" starts being used to mean "education" due to imitation of American usage.

English words are also "Spanglishized," as in *huacha* meaning "watch" or *bloque* to mean a cement block. Transliterations such as *"Dame quebrada"* for "Gimme a break" (even though *quebrar* means "break" only in the sense of "broken") give the *jerga fronteriza* (border jargon) a sort of pun structure transparent to the completely bilingual but mystifying to others. We include a

7

tiny fraction of this burgeoning vocabulary in this book but make no attempt at a comprehensive collection since it is not useful to travelers, fades off into Spanish and English slang so subtly, and changes too fast to nail down.

Cuando la suerte toca a tú puerta, nunca te encuentra.
Atentamente, De malas

Me siento en el agua sin mojarme.
La Sombra

I sit in the water without getting wet.
The Shadow

Los escultores viven en la edad de piedra.

Sculptors live in the stone age.

Mi Amor,
somos tan perfectos que no nos entendemos.
Atentamente,
Sra. Noche de Díaz

Más vale pájaro en mano que desear la mujer de tu hermano.

Linguistic and Pronunciation Notes

We assume that readers already have a basic command of Spanish. If not, get one before you run around spouting slang. The publisher of **Mexican Slang plus Graffiti** offers various books for learning basic Spanish on the order form at the back of this book; many books are available from a multitude of sources. Ordering **dos chelas** instead of **dos cervezas** is no big deal, and can give you the panache for which you probably purchased this book, but speaking more slang than Spanish will only make you look like an idiot.

Likewise, we assume you are familiar with Spanish pronunciation and are aware of gender endings. (If guys are **chavos**, chicks are **chavas**, if a bald man is **pelón** a bald woman is a *pelona*, old men are *viejitos*, old women *viejitas*, etc.) We also assume you can conjugate Spanish verbs, which are presented here in the infinitive form. (If not, just use the infinitives—you'll sound primitive, but will be understood.)

As far as pronunciation, remember that "ñ" is pronounced as "ny" in "canyon," "ll" is pronounced as "y." "J" is always pronounced as "h;" "h" is always silent, an initial "g" is pronounced as "h," unless followed by "u," in which case the diphthong is pronounced almost like "w." If a word ends in "l" or "r" it is accented on the last syllable. All other words are accented on the second to last syllable unless another syllable bears an accent mark. Vowels are simple, pure, and always pronounced the same:

a—as in "ah" or "mama"
e—like the long "a" in "make" or "way"
i—like long "e" in "feel" or "see"
o—as in "old" or "no"
u—without the initial "y" sound, as in "kudos" or "rude."

Chapter I

Translated Americanisms

The Labyrinth of "Golly, Dude!"

COOL: A major expression with many synonyms in both tongues.

Padre

Padre is the closest direct equivalent to cool. Carlos Colegiano says, *"Es cantante muy padre,"* (He's a really cool singer). It can be used impersonally, like "Far out!" *¡Ay, que padre!* Extremely cool would be *padrísimo*.

Curado

Similar to **padre** but hipper. Probably comes from the pun of **padre** meaning **cura** (priest). Omar Onda describes his new car as, *"Curado."*

Suave

While it means "smooth" or "soft," **suave** also has a definite equivalence to "cool" and **suavecito** is cooler yet. The Joe Camel "cool character" billboards in Mexico say **Un Tipo Suave**.

Chingón

A tougher, more masculine, street connotation, it could describe a car, motorcycle, or person and might be thought of as meaning "stud." Not polite, but highly visible on T-shirts and caps. Luis Angel Lambada says to Carlos Colegiano, *"Que coche más chingón"* (What a cool car.) Letícia Lambada agrees, *"Que machín,* (How bad.) **Machín** is a contraction of **más chingón**, the baddest or bitchin'est.

Chido

Chido means "cool" or "bitchin'," once gutter talk, but now a popular term with "yuppies." Beto Boca de Basura comments on Carlos' new wheels by saying, *"Chido, huey."*

Estar de Pelos

Hip, youth slang. Something like "rad" or "too much." Carlos Colegiano tells Conchita, *"La camisa está de pelos"* (The shirt is way cool.) A variation is *"pasar de peluche."* *Peluche* is fleece and *un osito de peluche* is a teddy bear. The very latest "Youthspeak" as we go to press is *"de pelos y jícamas,"* which was Omar Onda's reaction to the shirt.

Simpático

Means nice, especially of people. Nice people are also *bonito, lindo, buena onda, muy gente.* Conchita Colegiana says of Carlos, *"Él es gran tipo* (He's a great guy.) Olivia Onda agrees, *"¡Que tipazo!"* (What a guy!)

In fact, the use of the *-azo* ending, which implies a blow with or explosion of the word modified, is good for homemade slang. Olivia Onda summons a good-looking young waiter by calling, *"Jovenazo."* While Omar Onda, talks about greeting his girlfriend, Olivia, back from a long trip with a *colchonazo* (mattress attack).

Impersonally, *bonito* is literally the diminutive of "good," and means "nice." *Que bonito* is "How nice."

Caer Bien

To be *simpático*. *"Él me cae bien"* is the way Conchita Colegiana says "I like him," "He's all right," "He's cool with me." Reserve *me gusta* for things; use *me cae bien* when discussing people—especially people of the same sex.

Prendido

Prender means to turn on a light or light a fire, so something *muy prendido* is a real turn-on. Leticia Lambada describes chocolate ice cream, *"Me prende"* (it turns me on.) She's obviously a cheap date.

Bárbaro

Bárbaro means "barbaric," but, like the English "bad" can be either cool or uncool. As an exclamation *Que bárbaro* can mean "Way cool," "Far Out," etc. When Carlos brought Conchita Colegiana flowers she said, *"Que bárbaro,"* and kissed him.

But *"Que bárbaro"* or *Que barbaridad* (which comes from the same root) can mean "What a bummer" or "Disgraceful." When Carlos Colegiano tried to feel up Conchita and ripped her blouse she said, *"Que barbaridad,"* and slapped him.

Additionally, *una barbaridad de* means a lot of. Conchita explained to Carlos that the blouse *cuesta una barbaridad* (it cost an arm and a leg.) It's going to *costar una barbaridad de flores* for Carlos to get on Conchita's good side again.

Tranquilo

Means calm or serene, but is also cool in the sense of "cool it," "chill out," or calm down. Can be used as a one-word imperative. *Calmada* is similar to *tranquila* and *la cosa es calmada* or *todo calmado* means "everything's cool." *Tranquilo* can also mean "Take it easy," and is even used as a farewell in that sense.

Asombroso

Though it comes from the root *sombra*, shadow, it means what it sounds like: awesome.

UNCOOL

Gacho

Gacho is how Luis Angel Lambada says *feo* (ugly), but is used in a wider sense than in English. Road conditions, weather, behavior, music, can be *feo*, so it could mean "lousy," "in bad repair," etc. Used impersonally, *feo* has the sense of a drag, a bummer, "it sucks." Used about a person, it means ugly, unless applied to certain characteristics: *Tiene carácter feo* means "He's got a rotten character." *Gacho* is street slang and has all the same connotations. It can be used personally or impersonally; *¡Que gacho!* means "That sucks!" or "Bummer," or "What a drag." *Eres gacho* means "You stink." *No seas gacho* is "Don't be a drag" or "Come off it."

Omar Onda, Beto Boca de Basura and Luis Angel Lambada were watching girls on the corner when a really homely young woman passed by. *"Regularsona,"* said Beto. *"Federica,"* said Luis Angel. *"Química,"* said Omar, *"¡Porque no tiene nada de física!"*

Pesado

Literally means "heavy," but has a negative connotation in slang, very *antipático*. Generally applied to a person. Can mean boring, a drag, a creep. Also *pesadito*. Other terms include, *sangrón, peseta, caer en los huevos, chocante*. One frequently hears *No seas sangrón*, or *No seas pesado* for "Don't be a pain in the ass."

Chingado

Screwed up, jerked around, or simply fucked as in the T-Shirts that say *Estoy chingado*. When Beto Boca de Basura was making out with Leticia Lambada and got caught by Luis Angel he said, *"Estoy chingado."* *"¡Sangrona!"* was Luis Angel's reply.

17

Caer Gordo

Literally, "to fall fat," this is the opposite of *caer bien*. *"Ella me cae gorda,"* said Luis Angel after the incident; (I don't like her, she's a bummer, she rubs me the wrong way.) If you want to use an expression which is less slangy try *caer mal*.

Fuchi

Stinky, smelly. But by extension, anything corrupt, perverse, kinky, or not to the liking. As an exclamation, means "Phew!" or "Yuck!" Also *fu* or *furris*.

¡Guácala! (also spelled *wácala*) also means "Ugh!" "Yech!" "Gross!" or "Barf!" but is more about taste than smell. The comment is *de rigueur* when spitting something out on the floor.

FUNNY

Chistoso

From *chiste*—a joke. It means "funny" in the sense of comical, someone who jokes a lot. Other words for joke include *broma* (and the verb *bromear*) and *cotorro*. In Spanish, incidentally, there are no "dirty" jokes, but *chistes colorados* for "blue" material and *chistes verdes*, which are "sick" or off-color jokes. *Raspa* is a bad joke or pun (pun is *albur*, the verb *alburear*).

Gracioso

Also funny, as in "Very funny,"—*muy gracioso* or "What's so funny"—*¿Qué tiene de gracioso?* It can be a noun as in *¿Quién fue el gracioso?* (Who's the wise guy?); a humorous person; indicates natural humor or a practical joke rather than formally telling jokes.

Vaciado

Slang term, meaning funny in the sense of "a kick" or something that tickles one. *"¡Que vaciado que le gusta el rock a tu mami!"* (It's a scream that your mom likes rock music) commented Olivia Onda to Berta Boca de Basura. This word is not related to *vacilar*, to joke around.

Burlar

To joke or kid around. ***Burla*** is a joke, prank, or jest. It differs from ***chiste*** as telling a joke differs from a practical joke. Beto Boca de Basura likes to unscrew the top of the salt shaker in the restaurant so that when Luis Angel Lambada uses it, all the salt pours on his food. Beto is ***muy burlón***.

"You're kidding" is ***Me burlas***. "Don't put me on" would be ***No te burles***. A joker or "card" would be described as ***burlesco***.

Picarón

Picar means to sting or bite like a mosquito, but the word has wide application. "Hot" food, for example is ***picante***. *"¿Pica mucho?"* (Is this ***salsa*** very hot?) Berta Boca de Basura asks Beto. *"No,"* he assures her innocently.

There is also the use of ***pica*** in the sense of a bird's beak, and thus as a sobriquet for the penis. But a major use is in mention of joking and jesting—***picarón*** is a joker, a "card," the thing to call someone who's just put one over on you or told a good one.

The sense is more towards barbed or racy humor. *Picaresco* means a song with *letra picaresca,* a racy or sexy one.

Payasear

Fooling around, clowning around, kidding. *Payaso* means clown. "Just kidding" would be *Nomás estoy payaseando. No seas payaso* would mean "Cut the clowning."

"Payaso," Berta gasped accusingly to Beto after she tried the *salsa*.

Caer el Veinte

To "get" a joke can be expressed as *caer el veinte*, referring to the twenty *centavo* coins once used in telephones, and equivalent to our expression, "the coin finally dropped." *"Por fin le cayó el veinte,"* (she finally got it) said Omar Onda when Olivia laughed at last. *Caer* (to fall) by the way, is the way of expressing "fall for it." *No cayó* means "He didn't bite." *"¡Caíste!"* (You fell for it, Gotcha!) exclaimed Beto Boca de Basura, offering Berta some water.

Tomar los Pelos

Literally (taking the hair), this means "pulling my leg." *"¿Estás en serio o me estás tomando los pelos?"* (Are you serious, or are you pulling my leg?) asked Conchita Colegiana when the mechanic told her how much it would cost to fix her car.

Raro

The English use of "funny" to mean "odd" or "peculiar" does not follow in Spanish. "That's odd" would be *curiosa* and "weird" is *raro*. *"Esta sopa tiene un gusto raro,"* (this soup tastes funny) mumbled Beto Boca de Basura to Berta, wondering if she was trying to get back at him for the salsa incident. *Tipos raros* are strange people or weirdos.

GOOD-LOOKING

Guapo

All these words can be used with *bien* to mean "pretty cute," "really foxy," etc. *Guapo* is handsome, *guapa* is foxy. These can be used as an address: *"Hola, Guapo,"* (Hello, Handsome) Berta Boca de Basura greets Beto when he comes home, ready to make peace. *"Hay muchas guapas,"* (There are a lot of foxes around) Omar Onda tells Carlos Colegiano as they enter the party.

Other adjectives that can be feminized by changing the final "o" to "a" are *lindo, bonito,* and *buen mozo* (good looking). Only men are referred to as *cuadrado*—"built" or "buff."

Cuero

Carlos Colegiano calls good-looking women *cuero* (having a nice body or built,) *preciosa* or *mona* (cute), *chula* (pretty), *bella* or *hermosa* (beautiful), or *primorosa* (gorgeous). A beauty is *un primor,* or *una belleza.* Omar Onda calls good-looking women *cuerito* and *cuerazo,* *buenota, buena curva, guitarra* (from the shape of a guitar), or *mango.* Beto Boca de Basura calls good-looking women alley terms like *forro* and *forrazo.* After he's had a couple of drinks, Beto calls them *buen culito, buena percha* and *culo chido,* much ruder terms.

Sabrosa

Luis Angel Lambada has some cuter, racier adjectives for pretty women: *potable, sabrosa* (variations of tasty), *encamable, ensabanable* (bed-able), *revolcable* ("turnable-over"), and *mordisqueable* (toothsome, "nibble-able").

No Sabrosa

Perita en dulce (pear in syrup) can mean a "wannabe," or chick who thinks she's gorgeous. Ugly women are called *garra*, *piedra* (stone) or perhaps *pellejo* (rawhide or an animal skin).

BREAD, DOUGH

Feria

Most common slang for money in border areas is *feria*, which can mean "money" or "pocket change," depending. *No traigo feria* would indicate, "I don't have any change." Further south, one hears *lana*, which literally means "wool" but possibly is short for *porcelana*.

Plata

The term **plata** is understood to mean **dinero** throughout Latin America, but in Mexican border areas occasionally means **pesos** as opposed to dollars. Omar Onda asks *"¿Y cuánto en inglés?"* (How much in dollars?) Other words for money include **pachocha**, **luz**, and **marmaja**.

Con y Sin Lana

De lana means rich, so you hear odd phrases like **torta de lana** which means, not "wool sandwich," but a rich chick. Luis Angel Lambada says that Conchita Colegiana is *"una torta de lana."* Beto Boca de Basura agrees, adding that Carlos and Conchita are **ricardos** (rich).

Mendigo means "beggar," but when accented on the first syllable becomes a disparaging adjective similar to "damned" or a noun similar to "son of a bitch."

While **barata** is cheap, used as a noun it means a sale or bargain, as does **ganga**. Better yet would be **de balde** or **de oquis**, which mean "for free." **El enganche** (literally, hook) is a down payment or lay-away. **Abono**

25

·might be fertilizer but *en abonos* is installments or time payments (differing from *sistema de apartados*, which is "lay away") and would require an *enganche* (down payment). *Pilón* is a bonus, *laniap* or little gift, an incentive to do business with a particular shop. *"Doy pilón"* was Berta Boca de Basura's explanation when Beto accused her of giving him the clap.

Caifás is street slang for "pay up." *"Caifás con mi lana,"* (cough up my dough) Omar Onda said to Luis Angel Lambada. A similar phrase is *azota mi lana* (literally, "whip me my dough"). *Chambear* means "to work," *chamba* or *jale* mean job, or gig. A salary can be called *chivo* (he-goat) or *raya* (line or scratch), while a child's weekly allowance is his *domingo*.

Droga means "debt" as well as "drug," so terms like *droguero* and *endrogado* have secondary meanings of "heavy borrower" and "debt-ridden." *Apuro* is a financial bind *"Estoy en un apuro,"* Luis Angel told Omar. "Broke" can be *pelado* (peeled), *jorobado* (hunchbacked), or *brujo* (witch or sorcerer). *En la quinta* is to be in total poverty or misery, like "in the poorhouse."

GIMME A BREAK

Chanza

An almost literal translation would be the expression, *Dame chanza*. Street slang uses *Alviáname* to bum anything from cigarettes to favors. A similar usage is *mochate*, for mooching.

"No seas gacho, carnal. Alviáname. Mochate un frajo," (Be a sport, brother. Gimme a break. Spare me a cigarette) Luis Angel Lambada says to Beto Boca de Basura.

SHIT

Mierda

Mierda is the term and not used vulgarly as in English (where we use it for everything). *Miércoles* (Wednesday) is the slang term for doo-doo. *Caca* is the same in Spanish as in English, again without any other meanings. Also heard is *popó. Cagar* is the semi-crude verb for shitting used by Luis Angel Lambada, *zurrar* very crude word used by Beto Boca de Basura. So *cagón* and *zurrón* both mean "shit ass" or a shitty person. *Cagadero* means "crapper."

Miar is a cruder term for peeing than *orinar* and *mingitorio* is a pisser. Piss is also *chis* or *pipí*. *"Tengo que hacer pipí"* Olivia Onda tells Omar. *"Tiene chorro"* (crude for diarrhea) says Luis Angel Lambada. *"Tiene grifo"* (faucet; cruder for diarrhea) agrees Beto Boca de Basura.

"Bullshit" would be most politely translated as *mentiras* (lies), or perhaps the slangier *macanas* or *chucherías*. *"Déjate las macanas,"* (cut the crap) responds Olivia on her way to the bathroom. *Carambas* is used as a synonym in the since of "giving someone shit."

The term *basura* (garbage) is used more widely in Spanish and a mess, disaster, bad meal, or "piece of crap" would be a *porquería*, as would a messy house or room. *"¡Ay, que cochina!"* Conchita Colegiana reprimands the guys.

HIP, WITH IT

Cojonudo means "ballsy," but also means, "with it," as does the old expression *muy reata* (very lariat).

Oddly, while *muy acá* (real "here") means "hip" in most of Mexico, at the border and in the U.S. one hears *muy de aquellas* (real "there") to mean "way out" or "out of this world." Any of these expressions can be inflected to mean *creido* (believer), which is the Spanish way to say somebody thinks himself to be a big deal.

TOTALLY, TO THE MAX

Remate is an auction, but has a slang sense of "all the way." *Omar Onda es un loco de remate* (Omar Onda is a total nut). Another expression, *de hueso colorado* (red-boned) means dyed-in-the-wool, "totally," "last ditch," a diehard. It's often used to describe team fans or political partisans and a phrase like *Soy Mexicano de hueso colorado* is not too different from "red blooded American." Doing something "all the way out" or "full bore" is *a todo dar*, the slang version being *a todo madre*.

Al mal tiempo, buen paraguas.
Atentamente, Buenacara

El matrimonio puede llegar a ser un dúo o un duelo.

Marriage can become a duet or a duel.

Soy un desempleado con dos años de experiencia.

I'm unemployed with 2 years of experience.

La mejor maestra es la experiencia, siempre que tengas paciencia.

Experience is the best teacher, if you're patient.

Taxista que quiere ser libre, para taxista no sirve.
—Libertad

A taxi driver who wants to be free is no good as a taxi driver.
—Liberty

Por mucho madrugar aparecen las ojeras.

Early to bed and early to rise causes circles under your eyes.

Si estudian hace hombres grandes, que estudien los enanos.

Chiquito, pero picoso.

Small, but very spicy.

Chapter 2

Major Mexicanisms

Tengo madre muy padre, y padre de poca madre.

Madre

Madre is a very complex word in Mexico and produces quantities of rich slang. Without getting into the sociology of it, although the concept of Motherhood is held sacred in Mexico, *madre* means worthless, failed, a mess. *Una madre* is something unimportant, a put-down; *un desmadre*, is a total snafu. A *madrazo* is a heavy blow or jolt, a *madreador* or *madrino* is a bar bouncer, hit man, or goon (also *guarura*, bodyguard). *Partir la madre* is to smash, destroy, or bust something. The classic Mexican in-can insult (the equivalent of "Fuck you") is the famous *Chinga tu madre* or merely *Tu madre*.

Exceptions to all this maternal negativity are *a todo madre*, which means done right, superlative, done up brown, the whole nine yards; and *No tiene madre*—if something "has no mother" it is absolutely the coolest. However, and to illustrate the importance of context in such elemental slang, *Él no tiene madre* can also mean having no shame, so that *poca madre* is also a synonym for "jerk." Carlos Colegiano says, *Poca abuela* and thus avoids the crude use of the word *madre*).

Me vale madre, frequently seen on caps, shirts, and biker jackets, literally means "It makes mother to me," but is a direct equivalent to English expressions such as "I don't give a damn," or "Who gives a shit?" *Madre* used like this is considered crude speech and not acceptable in polite or mixed company, so there are euphemisms. Carlos Colegiano will say things like, *"Me vale M"* (as we would say, "the M word"). Omar Onda prefers to say, *drema*, and the similarly scrambled *la ingada chadre*.

Chingar

This is another major plexus of Mexicanisms, and more complex than most non-Mexicans think. *Chingar* does not mean precisely "Fuck," but comes from an older meaning of "rape" or "molest." While *No chingues con nosotros* is exactly equivalent to "Don't fuck with us," the famous *Chinga tu madre* is not sexual at all (worse, to a Mexican). Beto Boca de Basura exclaims, *"Hijo de la chingada* (son of a bitch, but in spades), *"Vete a la chingada"* (rougher than "go to hell," more like "get fucked.")

Hasta la quinta chingada means a long distance, "way the hell out," and can be shortened to *hasta la quinta.* A *chingazo* or *chingadazo* is a major blow or coup. *Chingadera* is a dirty trick. *"Me chingaron"* (I got screwed or jerked around—they did me), mourned Luis Angel Lambada. *No chingues* is "lay off" or "don't fuck around."

Chingón is a compliment—a stud, the guy who can *chingar* everybody else. *Un chingo de* means a whole lot of. Carlos Colegiano declares, *"Hace un chingo de años,*

Colón descubrió las Américas" (A whole heap of years ago, Columbus discovered America). The primacy of these *chinga* terms has led to a lot of expressions and ejaculations like *¡Chin!*, *¡Ay, Chihuahua!*, *¡Chispas!*, *¡Chicle!*, which are acceptable bailouts, just as we have all the "Gosh" and "Golly" words to prevent blasphemous use of "God."

Although *fregar* means cleaning or scrubbing in most Spanish countries, in Mexico it is a synonym for *chingar* in the sense of "messing with" or "bugging." *Fregado* means "snafued" or "screwed up" and *No me friegues* is "Don't bug me." A euphemism used in place of the various forms of *chingar* is *tiznar*.

La Onda

A constellation of hippy expressions which are still quite current. *Onda* means vibrations, so *¿Qué onda?* is something like, "What's the vibes?" and is the standard young, hip greeting, as ubiquitous as "What's happening?"

Buena onda, whether referring to a person or impersonal thing or event means "Good vibes." *"Ella es muy buena onda,"* (She's great people) Omar boasts of Olivia Onda. *"¡Que mala onda!"* (What a bummer!) he exclaimed when he heard she had broken her foot. Though not as often heard, *otra onda* can mean "something else" as in "Man, that band was something else."

Huevos

This is another complex Mexican term. The word means "eggs," but the reference to "balls" is so strong that you have to watch out using the word at all. Polite girls like Conchita Colegiana would order *blanquillos* from a male waiter. There are a raft of egg/balls puns and jokes.

Aside from the reproductive aspects, *huevo* means "lazy" for some reason, and is reflected in a complex of vulgar expressions like *huevón* (or *huevona*) as a synonym for *flojo* or lazy.

Luis Angel Lambada declares, "I failed for four reasons, *La Eva, la uva, el IVA, y el huevo.*" In other words, because of women (Eve), drink (the grape), taxes (the *Impuesto Valor Añadido*, or value added tax) and laziness. Though synonyms, **huevos** and **cojones** have different weights (see Chapter 4).

Puta

Means "whore," but is more extensively used than in English. This is what a Mexican would say if he hammered his finger. **Puta madre** is so much worse, a pretty close equivalent to the modern American use of "mother fucker." **Hijo de puta** means "bastard" or "son of a bitch," but worse.

Pedo

Pedo means "fart," plain and simple. To say it politely would be **un ventoso** or **echar un ventoso**. But the word is used in several special ways, none polite. **Huele-pedos** (a fart-smeller) is an exact equivalent of our "brown noser" (also termed **lamenalgas**—a butt-licker). **No hay pedo** means "no big deal." And **bien pedo** (really fart) means "blind drunk."

Cabrón

Is the main "bad noun," it literally means a big goat, but is used the way Americans use "ass hole" or "S.O.B." Can be fighting words, often "cleaned up" as *camión, camarón*, etc. It can be made diminutive to *cabroncito* and even *cabroncita*. *Un cabrón de siete suelas* (a seven-soled *cabrón*) is a "24 carat" ass hole. Also common is *cabrón de primera* (first class goat). A *cabronada* is the kind of thing a *cabrón* would do.

Cabronear, even in Mexico, means to be cuckolded knowingly and *cabronismo* is to prostitute one's own wife.

Pinche

Just as inexplicably, is the "bad adjective." Literally an assistant cook, means "nasty" and is used where Americans would say "fucking," "shitty," or what have you. "That fuckin' ass hole" would be *pinche cabrón* in Mexico.

Pues

Although the dictionary meaning is "since," *pues* (and it's colloquial variations, *pos* and *pus*) are slang expressions hard to translate but frequently used. It can be used like "Well..." at the first of a sentence (*Pues, no sé* is "Well, beats me") or as we would use "then" at the end of a phrase as in, *Ándale, pues*, (Go ahead, then) or as a general emphatic, perhaps like the New York use of "a'ready." An obvious question or statement can be answered, *Pos, sí*. A Tijuana *birriería* is called "*Guadalajara, Pues*," in the way an American deli might be called, "Brooklyn, Already."

Re-

The prefix *re-* has an escalating effect in slang, reminiscent of the California use of "way" to mean "very." Conchita Colegiana is *rebuena* (very good) and *recuero* (way stacked).

Leticia Lambada *es reloca* (She's really nuts). Even more emphatic, less used, is *rete-*. *"Te reteodio,"* (I hate your guts) she told Luis Angel when he forgot her birthday and went to the racetrack. *"Eres reteguapa,"* (you're ultra super foxy) Luis Angel told her; *"Te quiero siempre."* The ultimate lick is *requete-.* *"Estoy requeteseguro,"* (I'm absolutely certain) Luis Angel declared.

Mexicans use "super" as a similar prefix, as well. *Leticia estaba super-enojada*, (she was way pissed off). She didn't forgive him for a week.

EXCLAMATIONS

¡Hijole! is a super-Mexican expression that means things like, "Oh, wow!," "Holy cow!" or "Yikes!"

Sobres is enthusiastic agreement, like "Right on!," "Really," "You said it!" or "Yeah, let's do it!"

¡Chale! on the other hand, indicates disbelief as in, "Oh, sure," "No way," "Nice try" or "Tell me another one."

¡Ándale! is not only "Hurry up," but also "Get with it," "Get the lead out" and can mean either "Oh, go on with you!" or "Really!" as a reply to a statement.

¡Arriba (anything)! is like "up with" or "hooray for." Omar Onda points out the vast spiritual superiority of crying *¡arriba!* (up) instead of "Get down!"

¡Caramba! is famous, and can be about anything from "Wow!" to "Holy shit!" *Carambas* are also curses, hassles, and badmouthing in general.

¡Carajo! is a strong, violent oath.

Luis Angel Lambada likes to yell *"¡Mucha ropa!"* (a lot of clothes, take it off) at dancers or anyone in public. Sometimes it works.

¡Caray! is "Gosh!," "Wow!," "Holy cow!"

¡Zaz! or *¡Zas!* is like "Zap!," "Pow!," or "Oh, no!" This is cartoon language for the sound of blows.

Nam Nam is "Yum Yum."

"¡Águas! (a warning shout: Look out or Heads up) Carlos Colegiano yells when he and Beto are helping Berta move her furniture. Ghetto

slang for the same thing: *"¡Trucha!"* (trout) shouts Beto Boca de Basura. For some reason *trucha* is a warning that also has tones of "Jiggers!" or "Cheese it!"

"¡Arre!" (move it) Berta tells the boys; this has a special tone since the word means "Giddyup" to a burro (hence, a dunce).

Mi mayor aspiración es llegar a ser el número uno. El Cero

My greatest ambition is to be number one. - Zero

El que tiene miles sufre, él que debe millones goza.

Cuando el camino es corto, hasta los burros llegan.

Si el trabajo enorgullece, recuerda que el orgullo es pecado capital.

If work makes one proud, remember that pride is a mortal sin.

Yo hago como que trabajo, porque mi jefe hace como si me pagara. Asalariado.

I pretend to work because my boss pretends to pay me. Wage Slave

No existen balas capaces de matar nuestros sueños.

There are no bullets that can kill our dreams.

El amor ha hecho héroes, pero también idiotas.

Love has made heroes, but also idiots.

Si el estudio produce frutos ... que estudien los árboles. Atentamente, El Coco

If studying produces fruit ... let the trees study.

Las mujeres son como los frenos. Uno nunca sabe cuando se van.

Women are like brakes. You never know when they'll go out on you.

Cuando al fin encontré respuestas, me cambiaron las preguntas.

When I finally found answers, they changed the questions on me.

Chapter 3

People

No, **insurgente** doesn't mean "insult people"

Guys

Hombre is "Man," equivalent even as an ejaculation to "Oh, Man!" "Brother" to address a non-relative is not **hermano** but **'mano**. **Carnal** is like "Bro," but is likewise racially restricted except among extremely good friends. "Pal" would be **compadre**, more casually, **compa**, or at the slangiest, **compinche**. (Female equivalent, **comadre**, which has almost the sense of blacks using the term "sisters" or "sis."

Ese (literally, "that") is like "Hey, bud" and short for *ese vato*— "That guy" or "That cat," used as an attention getter like, "Hey, man," or "Hey, you."

Chico means "little one" or "kid." *Joven* means "youngster," or "young man," appropriate for calling a waiter or polite inquiries of younger males. *Mijo* (contraction of *mi hijo*, "my son") is like "sonny" and is for younger boys or affectionately with friends.

Other terms for friends (*amigos, compañeros*) are *socio* (partner), *parna, cuate* (often *cuaderno*, which really means notebook), *piojo* (louse), *valedor* (or *vale* for short).

Muchacho or *chico* are terms of reference for young men. *Tipo* means "guy." Also very common is *chavo*. The guys are *vatos* (also spelled *batos*), *cuates, amigotes*. *Fulano* is "whoever" or "so and so" and *fulano, zutano, y mengano* are Tom, Dick and Harry.

Chicks

Properly *muchachas, chicas* or more formally *señoritas. Mija,* is used in direct address the same as *mijo* with males. *'Mana* is "sister" and very commonly used form of address. *Chulis* is like "cutie," "honey," or "dearie"—often used between women (or male homosexuals). *Nena,* appropriate for little girls, can also be used affectionately for younger women, something like "kiddo" or "baby." Can also be used indirectly, *¿Quién es la nena aquella? Nenorra* can also be used as both indirect reference or direct address.

Mamacita is a definite come-on type of address, used like "Hey baby," to a girl passing on the street or affectionately between lovers; also *mamasota* or *mamuchis. Papacito* is the male equivalent, like "Daddy" used between lovers.

Indirect terms include, *tipa, chava,* and *morra,* all very common and acceptable terms, used by Carlos Colegiano. While Luis Angel Lambada calls women *torta,* a little sexist, but still basically means "chick."

Beto Boca de Basura calls them *Ruca*
which means "broad" in gutter talk
and is not at all polite.

Carlos Colegiano and Omar
Onda call mature women *puris, mur-
ciélagas* (bats), and *espátulas*. In the
alleys, Luis Angel Lambada and Beto
Boca de Basura call them *chundas,
fisgas* and *nacas*.

Lovers and Other Details

Los vatos on the street commonly refer to lovers (*amantes*) and
loved ones (*queridos*) as *huesos*, or as
vareda, pato, or *quelite*.

Affectionate and pet terms include *muñeca*, literally doll; *precio-
sura*, precious; *mi tesoro*, my treasure;
ricura, richness; and *chiquitín*, teeny
tiny. *Mi amor, mi vida*, and such are
used towards men and women. *Viejo*
is "the old man," or husband. *Papacito* or *mijo* are endearments towards men. Wives and lovers are often
referred to as *vieja* ("old lady," used
just like in English), or comically as
mi peor es nada, my "better than noth-
ing."

Carlos Colegiano and Omar Onda talk about their girlfriends (*novias*) as *detalles* (details), *cueros* (skins). Luis Angel Lambada talks about his *pescado* (fish), and Beto Boca de Basura, in the alley, calls his *catán*. All the guys refer to their love affairs (*aventuras amorosas*) as *volados, aguacates, volantines*, or *movidas*.

"To flirt" is properly *coquetear*, but in Mexico is also *volarse*. While *de volada* means "suddenly," *andar de volada* also means flirting. Other terms for flirting include *dar puerta* (giving the door), *dar entrada* (giving out tickets), *pelar los dientes* (peeling the teeth), *hacer el iris* (making the iris), *mover el agua* (stirring the water), and *levantar polvo* (raising dust). "Before she met Omar, *Olivia levantaba polvo con los chavos,*" (She was always flirting with the boys) Conchita Colegiana told Leticia Lambada. "*Sí. Ella siempre daba entrada a los guapos,*" Leticia agreed.

Kids

There are a lot of words to use instead of *niños*. Most mean simply "small," like *chico, chiquito*, or

47

pequeño. There are a lot of regional slang terms for kids, like the Mexican *chamaco*, the central American *guagua*, the Argentine *pibe*.

Babies (*infantes, bebés*) are often called *bambinos* in Mexico. Other regional slang includes *buki* (as in the famous Mexican singing group "*Los Bukis*").

Educación means "upbringing," not "education" in Spanish. *Ay, que niño más bien educado*, means "What a well brought up child." A less well-behaved kid can be referred to as *travieso* (misbehaving) or *escuintle* (brat), *mocoso* (snot-nosed). "Spoiled" is *malcriado* and *chiquiado* means "babied" or "treated like a little kid."

Fresa originally meant straight-laced or one who would not smoke pot. Since the popular song about the *Niña Fresa* it is used to describe coddled kids and teenagers. You also hear the word *fresa* (strawberry) applied to brats, and also to dandies, like yuppie fashion plates.

Mexicans use the word *ranchero* for "shy." So Omar Onda says *"No seas rancherita,"* to a little girl hiding behind her mother's skirts.

Parents and Elders

Parents are *padres* in Spanish; *parientes* refers to all relatives, as does *familiares*. Carlos Colegiano refers to his parents as *mis jefes* (my bosses).

Jefa is both "mother" and "old lady" in the conjugal sense, like *vieja*. *"Juro por mi jefecita"* (I swear by my old lady) Omar Onda assures Carlos. Carlos and Omar use other slang words for *madre* including *mandona, venerable, sarra, and margarita*. Street cant, used by Beto Boca de Basura and Luis Lambada includes *angustiosa* and *angustiada* (anguished).

Primo means cousin, but is also used to mean "naive"—a hick or chump, someone who has *cara de gringo* (the face of a Gringo).

Suegra means "mother-in-law" (with all the same jokes and bumper stickers we have), and is frequently heard as *suegrita*.

Abuela (grandmother) is almost always used in the affectionate diminutive (*abuelita*, like "granny"). Mexican kids use *Tu abuelita* in insults much like American kids use "your mama." While one doesn't use *viejo* or *vieja* to refer to mom or dad individually, *los viejos* is "the old folks."

Less kind terms for old women (*ancianas*) are *rucas, rucasianas, reliquias* (relics), *mómias* (mummies), *muñeca de antaño* (doll from yesteryear) *veteranas*. Some joking terms include the punning *Venus de mil ochocientos* (Venus from 1800), *de cuando el árbol de Noche Buena estaba en maceta* (from when the first Christmas tree was in a pot), and *cuando la Sierra Madre era señorita* (when the Sierra Madre range was a virgin).

Personal Characteristics

Many Spanish words describing people's physical and behavioral traits can be formed from root words by adding suffixes; either "*...ón*" or "*...udo*" meaning "much given to." Thus words like *llorar* (cry), *boca* (mouth), or *barriga* (belly), become *llorón*—and *llorona*, of course—(crybaby), *bocón* (bigmouth), and *barrigón* (potbellied). Similarly, *piernas* (legs), *bigotes* (mustaches), and *pelo* (hair) can transform to *piernuda* (having shapely legs), *bigotudo* (having a mustache), and *peludo* (hairy).

Remember that in Spanish most adjectives can be used as nouns. Omar Onda and Luis Lambada were comparing women passing by. *"Ella es muy piernuda"* (She has great legs), Omar asserted of one. *"Mira aquella peluda"* (Look at that hairy chick), Luis pointed out. These are equally correct usages.

Other such terms include:
comelón—a glutton or piggish
cabezón—big-headed
nalgona—woman with big butt
ojón—bug-eyed
panzón—pot-bellied
pelón—shave-headed or bald
tripón—chubby or tubby
trompudo—having big lips

Latins are quite given to calling each other by such nicknames. Any group will include people called

Gordo (Fats), *Flaco* (Slim), *Güero* (Whitey), *Chaparro* or *Chaparrito* (Shorty), and *Chato* (Snub-nose).

Other characteristics: Curly hair is called *pelo chino* for some reason, and curls are *chinos*. *Metiche* means "nosy," a "buttinsky" (from *meter* to stick in). *Hocicón* from *hocico* (snout), means talkative, a "jaw jacker." *Catrín* means "dude," in the sense of a dandy or "high hat." The kind of person likely to be found in places of *mucho postín*, swank, plush spots. *Comodín* is a sharpie or trickster. *Gorrón* means a moocher or chisler, somebody who's always putting on the bite. *Pediche* means the very same thing.

Quarrelsome people are *lión* (from *lío*, a fight), *bravero, muy pavo* (very turkey*) resalsa*, or *muy nalga* (real butt). *Ruco*, meaning "old" is also seen as *racalín* in the affectionate or teasing sense.

Insults

We mentioned *cabrón*, the kind of word men are always calling their friends in mock insult (as well as applying in genuine insult). Next most common would be *buey*, a fairly harmless word meaning ox. But for some reason when pronounced as *guey* or *wey* (as it often is), it becomes a harsher word, not for polite company but the kind of word with which Beto Boca de Basura and many other street-types end every phrase.

Pendejo is a very Mexican expletive, a poorly defined synonym for jerk (but originally coming from "pubic hair") and not-acceptable in polite company. *Pendejos* are known for committing *pendejadas*. All of these words are unisex.

Absolutely **the** most vulgar word for pussy is *verijas,* which is **never** used affectionately as other sometimes insulting words can be. It is possibly the most taboo word in Mexico in this day and age, possibly in all of Latin America. Therefore, the greatest possible insult (and we will not be responsible in any way, shape or form if you choose to use this word) is (drum roll, please) *verijona*. Caution: use this information with care.

Synonyms for "stupid" abound and all can be converted to the desired gender: among them are the easily recognizable *crétino, idiota, imbécil* (a unisex word), and *estúpido.* Be careful, this is stronger in Spanish than in English and many Mexicans, particularly women, don't like being called *estúpida* even in fun. *Tonto* (fool), *menso* (female is *mensa*, much to the chagrin of members of the high IQ group), and *jetón* are a few more. *Baboso* is a good one, frequently heard, and comes from a root meaning "to drool" and is therefore a drooling idiot.

Noteworthy is the Spanish construction by which *por* is used to mean "because of" or "on account of." Playful constructions we have heard include:

Me encarcelaron por feo (they locked me up for being ugly).

Fracasé por pendejo (I failed because I was a dumb jerk).

Toma, por egoísta (take that for being selfish).

Se busca por tonto (wanted for stupidity).

¡Al fin veo una pared limpia!

At last, a clean wall!

Chapter 4

Sex

Fuck

Polite terms would be *hacer amor* or *tener relaciones sexuales*, euphemistic would be *acostar con* (go to bed with). Standard rude is *coger*, which is an equivalent of "to fuck" (though it really means "catch," so use with care).

Another term is *joder*. This is especially common in the sense of *"No me jodas,"* (don't fuck with me) Luis Angel Lambada told Beto. *"Está jodido,"* (all fucked up) Luis said when he let slip to the girls that the guys were planning a stag party. Extremely crude (hinting at sodomy) is *culear. "Culeaste todo,"* Beto Boca de Basura yelled at Luis Angel. (Mexicans have no expressions equivalent to "Fuck you.")

Fajar means heavy petting, making out, derived from *fajas* (girdle or shirttail). "A fuck" is *una cogida.* *Curar*, (to cure) can mean screwing: *Cúramelo* (cure me of it) is a sexual come-on. *"Cúrame, mamacita,"* begs Omar Onda when he and Olivia park to *fajar.*

Suck

Mamar (to suck) is common and *Mámame* means "Suck me off." The addition of a single letter M has changed many loving graffiti (*Omar ama a Olivia*) to ribald descriptions of intimacy (*Omar mama a Olivia*). *Chupar* also means "to suck" and you hear *chupa la verga* for "suck my dick." A blow job is *una chupada* or *una mamada. No mames*, means "Don't bug me" or "Lay off."

Penis

Polite is *pene.* Crude is *la verga* (a ship's yard arm), often used as an oath or ejaculation by itself. A hard-on is called *verga dura* or a *parado* (because it stands). This word makes the sign on buses, *Precaución, paradas continuas*, a bit of joke).

Extremely common is *chile*, a source of many puns. *Chiludo* would mean "well hung." Among the inevitable multitude of others, some common terms for the *partes nobles* are:

pájaro ("bird," another source of puns and jokes)

pito (whistle)

pirinola

pinga (a general purpose word like "dick")

picha

bastón (cane)

bastardo

carnada (bait)

camote (sweet potato)

chóstomo comical, not too common

perno (spike)

pistola

rifle (sources of yet more puns)

chorizo (pork sausage)

elote (corncob)

hueso (bone)

el explorador

guía adelante (the forward guide)

pipí (for a tiny one)

Another term, *lechero* (the milk-man) comes from the Spanish use of the word *leche* (milk) to describe semen or "cum."

Vagina

Polite term is *vagina*. The most common crude term, equivalent to pussy, is *panocha*, which normally means unrefined brown sugar. *Panocha* may be an insult, or even a term of affection. Another major term is *pucha*, which in Argentina means merely "drat." The most taboo bad word in Mexico, *verijas*, means vagina. Others include:

la cucaracha (cockroach)
sartén (skillet)
lunar peludo (hairy birthmark)
nido (nest, for *pájaros*)
mamey
bizcocho (biscuit)
pepita
mondongo
paparrucha
concha (sea shell)
tamal
paloma (dove)
pepa
araña (spider)
chango (monkey)

oso (bear)

papaya; No es lo mismo una papaya tapatía que ¡Tápate la papaya, Tía!

Argolla (a washer) is a slang term for the hymen, similar to "cherry." *Traer caballo* (to ride on horseback) means to menstruate as in *Ella no pudo, porque traía caballo* (She couldn't because she was on the rag).

Tits

The politest term is *senos*. The breast is properly called *pecho*, breasts are often called *pechitos*. "Tits" is most directly equivalent to *chichis* or *chichornias*, and a busty woman is a *chichona*. Mexico City slang is *repisas* (shelves). Other terms are *chimeneas* (chimneys), *peras* (pears), *agarraderas* (subway hand straps), *alimentos* (food, nourishment), *defensas* (bumpers), or *educación "Ella tuvo una buena educación,"* Omar Onda commented to Carlos Colegiano about Conchita.

Ass

Mexicans call the butt *las nalgas* (buttocks), or the slangier *nachas*. A cutsier term like "booty," more used by women, is *pompis*. "Tail" is *cola*. The anus is *ano*, so the importance of placing the tilde (the squiggly line over the ñ) becomes obvious. Asshole is *cono*; both *ano* and *cono* are more popularly expressed as *culo*. The anus is also referred to as *el chico, el polo sur* (the South Pole), and *ojete*, commonly written phonetically as *OGT*.

Mexicans don't call people "ass holes" like we do, although one hears *culero*, which has a sense of "coward" about it, one who shows his anus when running away. Obviously many English expressions don't translate, like "kick ass," "I'm after your ass," "piece of ass," and so forth.

A spanking is a *nalgada*. *Trasero* means "rear end" or "butt" and a shapely female behind is often called *diferencial* (a car's rear end). The term *mapa mundi* (world map) is used to mean a view of the *derriere*, similar to the English slang term "moon."

A cute expression for *culo* is *cucu*, and a popular party song is "*No Te Metas Con Mi Cucu*." Good for laughs is to convert the lyric to *mi rucu*, which subtly adds the concept of *ruco* or "old," especially my old lady.

Balls

In addition to the ubiquitous *huevos*, the gonads, properly *criadillas* or *testículos*, are called *cojones, cuates, óvalos, bolas*, or in alley talk, *obstáculos*. *Huerfanos* (orphans), *tanates* and *aguacates* (avocados) are also heard, the last two probably being precolumbian in origin. *Cojones* is most often used as "balls" in the sense of bravery or brashness and *tener cojones* (like *tener tripas*) means "having guts." *Cojonudo* is "ballsy" and a hell of a fellow.

Doing It

Though of limited utility, these expressions for "getting it on" are so colorful we knew you'd want to know them: *bastardear, echar un palo* (throw the stick), *medir su aceite* (check her oil), *darle a comer al chango* (feed the monkey), *revisar los interiores* (examine the interior), *subir al guayabo* (climb the guava tree), *andar por caderas* (walk on the hips), *mojar el barbón* (wet the bearded one), *tomar medidas por dentro* (take inside measurements), *tronar los huesitos* (rattle the bones), *aplicar inyección intrapiernosa* (give an intra-leg injection), *reunir los ombligos* (join bellybuttons). Two cutsie expressions for "making it" are the *cuchi-cuchi* or *riqui-riqui*. More local color: to deflower a woman is *hacer un favor* (do a favor), *tronar el parche* (blow the patch), *romper el tambor* (rip the drum), *dejar sin cosita*, and *descorchar* (uncork).

Masturbation

Hacer la chaqueta (making the jacket) or *chaquetear* are by far the most common expressions. Others for male self-service often involve variations on *puño* (fist). Hence *puñetazo* and *hacer la puñeta* (making like a pump shotgun). One also hears *paja* (straw) and *hacer paja* to mean "jacking off." A *puñetero* or *pajero* is therefore a chronic masturbator or jackoff. Female self-service (and finger-fucking in general) is *dedear* (fingering).

Heavy Petting

When caresses (*caricias*) and hugs (*abrazos*) get specific they are called other things. *Sobas* are hugs, but *sobar* also applies to all degrees of petting. *Apapachar*, for instance is to "cop a feel" and *chichonear* means to fondle the breasts. *Dedear* is to finger whatever parts with an eye to *cachondear* (sexually excite). A person thus made *cachondo* has *ansias* or "the hots." Another term is *soplar*, in this sense meaning to get hot, usually said of women. Someone with chronic "hots" is said to be *caliente*. That's why it's such a giggle when those just learning Spanish translate directly from English and say *"Estoy caliente"* instead of *"Tengo calor."* *Fajar* is also making out or petting.

Empelotado means both naked and madly in love or moonstruck (which could also be said *locamente enamorado* or *encadicalo*). Naked is also *desnuda* or *encuerado*. *Encuérate* means "get naked." *Hazme piojito* (make me a louse) means "Scratch me on the head."

Pregnant

Unfortunately (though sometimes appropriately, no doubt) *embarazada* is the word for both pregnant and embarrassed. This can be clarified by using *encinta* or *esperando un bebé* for the first case and *pena* or *me da pena* for embarrassment or "He embarrassed me." *En estado* and *enferma* are also ways to indicate that a woman is with child. *Coneja* is a woman who is always "knocked up." There is further confusion since *aborto* means both an abortion and a miscarriage though *abortaje* is always the former. Abortionists are called *espantacigüenas* (stork-scarers) or, extremely crudely, *cuchareros* (spooners). Childbirth is a *parto*, by the way, and a midwife or obstetrician is a *partera*.

Homosexual

Among the inevitable swarm of words and innuendo the polite and correct term is *homosexual*. A light, joking term similar to fairy or flit is *lilo*. The standard term, not completely polite but acceptable, is *joto*. A harsh term, comparable to faggot would be *puto* (masc. of *puta*, whore). *Putón* is a flaming faggot. Many

Americans know *maricón*, (or *marica*, the same word) which can be used as a synonym for gay, but actually means "sissy" or "effeminate." *Volteado* (turned around) or *invertido* (upside down) also describe male homosexuals. *Vestida* is a male transvestite.

The female equivalent, like "butch," would be *marimacha*. With women, the correct term would be *lesbiana*. *Tortillera* is a lesbian and *hacer tortillas* is what they do. The word "gay" is used in Mexico, though the pronunciation is often "Spanishized" to sound like the English word "guy."

Both male and female homosexuality are "41," or *cuarenta y uno*. Reason is unsure, but possibly because it is the reverse of 14 or *catorce*, which means "sex" or "fuck." Incidentally, in Spanish countries AIDS is *el SIDA* and those with AIDS are *sidosos*.

Kinky

This word doesn't have many Spanish equivalents other than prosaic ones like *pervertido* or *aberraciones sexuales*. Most terms like *invertido* and *volteado* (turned over) refer to homosexuality and most English technical terms transliterate (*masoquismo, sadismo, fetichismo*, etc.), However the expression *de los otros* ("of the others") denotes deviation and *aves raros* can also refer to kinky persons.

Promiscuity

As in English, there is a wide range of judgmental terms for female promiscuity. In between *juilona* (a loose, gadabout girl) and *puta* (an outright whore), are *coscolina* (slut) and *piruja* (a "pro/am" slut), while *resbalosa* is a tease. *Sarrastra* is a woman of worst possible morals and reputation.

Amasia is a kept woman or mistress (and can also be *amasio*). *Amasiato* is a common-law mate. Common-law marriage is so common in Mexico that government forms have a box to check for *soltero/a* (single), *casado/a* (married), *divorciado/a* (divorced), *separado/a* (separated), and *union libre* (free union or common-law union).

On the male side of the ledger, *mujeriego* or *mujereo* is a womanizer (the female equivalent would be *hombreriega*. *Birriondo* means a stud or cocksman, *chichonero* is a "tit man"and *garañón* is an animal at stud, and thus a loose male or wolf, though the normal Mexican term for "wolf" is *tiburón* (shark). A *congalero* (from *congal*—bordello) is a whore-hopper or sexual low life.

Lower yet is to *gatear*—household servant girls, generally from low, uneducated classes, are called *gatas* (cats) and to pursue them sexually is to *gatear* which means "crawl" in a different context.

THE DEMIMONDE

For purely sociological reasons, we present a list of terms used in "red light" areas:

Condom

Simple safety requires a knowledge of technical terminology. "Rubbers" are properly called *condón*, or *preservativo* (a telling word in this day and age), they are also known as *diablito*, *portalápiz* (pencil box), *doña*

Prudencia, sombrero de Panamá, paraguas (umbrella), *impermeable* (raincoat), *globito* or *bomba* (both words meaning balloon), *caperucita en carnada* (caped bait), or *desafinador* ("untuner").

Prostitute

Formally *prostituta*, often shortened to *prosti*, a whore is called a *puta*. There are many other terms, like *lionas*, (quarrelsome), *araña* (spider), *gallina* (hen), *ratera*. *Talonera* and *piruja* are also common. A streetwalker is a *callejera*, a pushy one is a *garrapata* (lit. grabs-your-paw, a tick), and an ugly one, a *gaviota* (sea gull).

Brothel

There are a lot of prudish terms like *casa non sancta, casa de citas, casa de mala nota*, but a *burdel* is usually called a *putero* or a *congal*. Some street terms are *bodio, zumbido, cortijo, manflota*, and *bule.*

"B Girls"

Terms for *cabareteras* include the common *fichera* (girls who are paid for tokens or *fichas* they get for drinks sold at their tables), *linas, peseras, ratoneras, exprimidoras*. They could also be exotic dancers (*bailarinas*), of course, or strippers (*vedéttes*—pronounced in French style— or *encueratrices*).

Madame

Madre Superiora (mother superior) and *abadesa* (abbess) have a spurious religious ring to them. *Madrina, madrota, doña de las naguas* (lady of the petticoats), or *jefa de relaciones públicas* (head of public relations).

Pimp

Properly *tratante de blancas* (trader in white women), they are also called *putañero, padrote, cinturita*, or *fundillero* (the latter from *fundillo*, the anus). "Procurer" is also *alcahuete* and, for that matter *alcahueta*.

General Sex Pistols

The word *sexy* is used in Mexico. Horny is most usually *caliente* but one also hears *jadeoso*, literally "panting." A "quickie" is *un rapidín*, and a "nooner" is the Spanish word for matinee, *tardeada*. Mexicans also use "come" in the sexual sense and *ve-*

nirse juntos means to come together in both senses. In the reflexive, *venir* almost always means to climax: *Me vine* means "I came." Another way to say it would be *Me gocé* (I enjoyed myself). There is a phrase *el mismo orgasmo*, which means "the most," "the main event."

Cute for panties is *chones* and, even cuter, *choninos*. "Crabs," or lice are *piojos*, *chatos*, or *ladillas*.

Mexicans are very big on the concept of "horns," of being cuckolded. To *poner cuernos* (put horns) on someone is to have carnal knowledge of his wife. (Reverse "horning" is not mentioned or at least not named.) A cuckold is a *cornudo* (and would jokingly be called *Cornelio*.) "*Sancho*" is an interesting character, the personification of the person who comes in and puts horns on hubby while he's away. There are songs about *Sancho* (and also *Sancha*).

OGT

Se están
acabando los
genios ...
Beethoven se
quedó sordo,
Einstein se murió,
y a mí me está
doliendo la cabeza.

The great
geniuses are
ending ...
Beethoven went
deaf, Einstein
died, and I'm
getting a headache.

Mi hermana se tomó unos tragos y se le subieron.

Si la barba fuera signo de inteligencia, la cabra sería Sócrates.

If beards were a sign of intelligence, the nanny goat would be Socrates.

No hay honradez que resista tentación de cien millones.
Atentamente, Político Honrado.

There is no honor that can resist the temptation of a hundred million.
Sincerely, An Honest Politician

Hay soldados tan brutos que tienen que hacer curso de inteligencia.

There are soldiers so stupid that they have to take a course in intelligence.

El matrimonio puede llegar a ser un dúo o un duelo.

Marriage can become a duet or a duel.

Chapter 5

Drugs

Just say, "¡No way, José!"

Marijuana

Mota means "pot," the main word used in most places, with *yerba* or *hierba* (herb) a close second. But as in English, there are many colorful terms. Some are just puns on *mota*, like *motocicleta* or *motivosa*. Others are nicknames and brand names like *clorofila*, *grifa*, *de la verde*, *de la buena*, or *fina esmeralda*. Unlikely to be heard by an outsider, but sufficiently colorful to be shared, are: *coliflor tostada* (toasted cauliflower), *orégano chino* (chinese oregano), *zacate inglés* (English hay), *doradilla* (little golden), *doña diabla* (devil lady), *dama de la ardiente cabellera* (lady

73

of the flaming hairdo—for the red stamens of the weed), *nalga de ángel* (angel's butt), *trueno verde* (green thunder), and *motor de chorro* (jet engine). Also heard are *mora, mois,* and *café*.

Mexican "heads" (*marihuanos*) say *quemar* (burning) or *tostar* (toasting) instead of smoking. Other terms include, *motorizar* (motorize, but a pun on *mota*), *dorar* (gild, fry or toast golden brown), *enyerbar* (to herb), *grifear*, and the poetic *enamoriscar*, a hybrid of *enamorar* (to fall in love) and *mordisquear* (to nibble). Stoners are known as *grifo, motorolo* or *macizo*.

A "hit" or "toke" is an *acelerón*. There is a colorful selection of words for "joint," including *cigarro, churro, chumo, pito, pris, dubi* and the street term *porro*. The most common in the D.F. is *toque*. The roach or butt is *bachicha* or *bacha* and the roach clip is a *matabachas*. Beto Boca de Basura said to Luis Angel Lambada, *"Oye grifo, vamos a tostar un porro." "Simón, 'mano. Motorizamos. Pero no invitamos a Carlos*

Colegiano—es una fresa," (lit. strawberry, but means straightlaced, someone who doesn't smoke pot.)

An interesting etymology here: "Your turn" in Spanish would be *Te toca* or *Tu toque*. Start passing one around in Mexico and it suddenly becomes clear where a silly word like "toke" came from. It's just how one tokes over the line. To be stoned is *pasado, pacheco, hasta atrás, pastel, hasta la madre, hasta las chanclas,* and so on. The *hasta* — expressions are also applied to being drunk on liquor as well as high on weed or drugs.

Alcohol

See "Party Time," in chapter seven.

Cigarettes

Frajo is common street slang, especially in the North. *Chilango* street slang is *menurrón*. One also hears *cartucho* or *tambillo*. Old timers still say *un chiva*. A cute local equivalent for "coffin nails" is *tacos de cáncer*.

Others

Cocaine (*cocaína*) is called *coca* on the street, oddly also what you ask for when ordering a Coca-Cola. Presumably confusion will be minimal. Heroin (*heroína*) is called *chiva* by traffickers (*traficantes*, *narcos* or *drogueros*).

Other terms for opiates include, *nieve* (snow), *cura* (meaning both "priest" and "cure"), *tecata*, *medicina*, *doña blanca* (white lady). Opium and brown heroin from Mexico are sometimes called *chicloso de mandarín* (Mandarin chewing gum), *chocolate chino* (chinese chocolate) or, more commonly, *Chinaloa* (Sinaloa being a major producing state). Around the border, one is occasionally offered *Sherm*, which is PCP in case you'd like to avoid that experience.

Saint for Sale

When traveling in Mexico, you may see roadside shrines to *Jesús Malverde*. This is the patron saint of *traficantes*, although probably not recognized by the Roman Catholic church. Whether you stop to light a candle or not might depend on your line of work and how many *federales* are around at the time.

You're probably expecting all sorts of warnings and disclaimers about drugs, so why should we bother? Suffice it to say that an acquaintanceship with drugs in Mexico or Latin American can quickly put one on a first name basis with The Law, so here are some helpful terms to while away the time.

CRIME AND PUNISHMENT

Cops

The *policía* or *patrulla* are most often called *placas* (badges) on the streets instead of *oficial*. An underground *Chilango* term is *garfil*.

There are also many terms like *azul*, *tamarindo*, *jaiba*, *chocolate*, and *chocomilk* that derive from the color of their uniforms and some terms for traffic cops (like *lobo* or *feroz*) that derive from the natural hatred for the cops that hit them up for the *mordida* (bribe) on the road. A cop much given to the "take" is a *mordelón*.

Being arrested (*aprehendido,* *arrestado, detenido*) is called by verbs like *agarrar* (grab), *torcer* (twist), *rodar* (roll), and the alley-wise *aparuscar* or *amacizar*. Or *"Me preguntaron, pero no me invitaron,"* (They questioned me, but didn't "invite" me) as a mystified Beto Boca de Basura explained to Berta; *"Tal vez Carlos me puso el dedo,"* Beto said thoughtfully. The "paddy wagon" is *júlia*.

Jail and Prison

Terms for jail (*cárcel, calabozo*) or prison (*penitenciaría, prisión*) are many. Jail is often called the *tambo* or *bote* and a very common street term for prison (or *la peni*) is *la pinta*, derived from the expression *hacer pinta* (to play hookey from school).

Stealing

Street terms for *robar* include *borrar* (erase), *bajar* (lower), *pegar* (hit), *cleptomanear, pelar* (peel), *carrancear*, *birlar* and *trabajar con fé* (work with faith—applied to burglarizing). Thieves, properly *ladrones* or *rateros* are called *uñas* (fingernails) or *ratones* (rats) on the street. A common hand signal is, with the hand palm-down, to close the fingers as if picking up something; coupled with a glance toward the *ratero* a friend silently tips off another of the presence of a known thief.

To "squeal" is *soplar* (blow) and a "snitch" is a *rata* or *soplón*. To snitch someone off is to *poner rata* or *poner el dedo*. There is a cute song, popular on the radio, in which the chorus complains *"La vecina me puso el dedo."*

Yo era modesto,
pero lo superé.
Ahora soy perfecto.

I was modest, but I
got over it.
Now I'm perfect.

M x 9 = A
Matrimonio x Interés = Aburrido

Mi única infidelidad es pensar en ti cuando tú no estás.

My only infidelity is to think about you when you're not here.

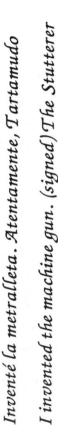

Inventé la metralleta. Atentamente, Tartamudo

I invented the machine gun. (signed) The Stutterer

La suegra buena es la suegra muerta. Atentamente, Yerno Feliz

Sí hay romanticismo, lo que no hay son buenos sueldos. Atentamente, Desempleado

Chapter 6

Rock and Roll

Actually, most hip Mexican rock slang is merely English. You won't need translations to speak of "punk," "heavy metal," "rap," "jazz," "blues," "country" or "rock" music. Those wishing to explore Mexican music might ask about *ranchero* or *norteño* (cowboy, country music), *cúmbia* or *música tropical* (infectious Caribbean boogie music), *baladas* (ballads), or *bailables* (dance music).

Disco is both a record and a discotheque, a *discoteca* is a record store. "Hits" are *éxitos* or *pegaditos* hit music is *música de mucho pegue*. To play music in Spanish is *tocar*.

Along with *música rock*, there are words like *rocanrolero* (a rocker, as in the Timbiriche hit, *El Gato Rocanrolero*) and *roquear* meaning to rock, as in the expression *roqueándote toda la noche* (rocking you all night long). An expression almost sure to get a laugh is *"¡Queremos rock!"* (We want rock), a tag line of a famous television comedian.

While *cine* is "the movies," by the way, "film" is *película* and *de película* means "fabulous," like something out of a movie. *Toda la película* (the whole movie), on the other hand, means "the whole nine yards," "the whole song and dance," "the works."

Si la vida te da penas págale con consoladores.

La verdad no peca, pero pica.

Las mujeres lloran antes del matrimonio,
los hombres después.
Women cry before the wedding, men after.

Chapter 7

Party Time

You mean *birria* really is Spanish for "beer"?

Party

F*iestas* are parties, all right, but the term more often used for partying down is *pachanga*, and "to party" is *pachanguear*. A *pachanguero* is a "party animal" and "party doll" or "party girl" would be *nena pachanguera*. Also used are *reventón* (literally, a "blowout") or *reve* for short. A *parranda* or *francachela* is a drunken spree or orgy, *tertulia* a dance party, and *frasca* or *fracas* an impromptu bash. A special fancy is the *lunada*, a moonlight party, often at the beach if there's one nearby.

A *borrachera* is a drunken bash, and when combined with *boda* (wedding) yields the popular pun "*bodachera*" to mean a very wet wedding.

Eating

Slang terms for *comer* include: *filiar*, very big in the capital, and *empacar* (pack). Other ways of saying, "Tie on the feed bag" include: *menear la quijada* (wiggle the jaw), *mover el bigote* (move the mustache). *Hambre* (hunger) can also be *ambrosia, filo* or *filomeno*. "I'm hungry," is *Tengo ambrosia* on the streets.

One hears *tortillas* called *gordas, guarnelas, guarnetas, sorias, discos* and, among the with-it, *long pleis*. Instead of *frijoles*, beans are sometimes called *balas, balines, parque, los completadores, chispolitos*, or the street word, *parraleños*.

Drinking

While the verb to drink is technically *beber*, everyone really says *tomar*. The waiter asks, "*¿Algo de* *tomar?"* (Anything to drink?) and the cop asks, *"¿Estabas tomando?"* (You been drinking?).

A drink, as in "Lets have a drink," is *un trago* from *tragar*, to swallow or gulp. Drinks are also referred to as *copas*, technically stemmed glasses. Oddly, while *jalón* (a pull) means a "snort," *empujar* (push) means to drink steadily. "Shots" or "belts" of booze are also termed *farolazos* (beams from searchlights) and *fajos* (fistfuls).

Slangier words for imbibing are *infle*, *libar*, and *chupar*. The latter is quite common and means "suck," so *Vamos a chupar unas chelas* means "Let's go suck some suds." You could also say, *Vamos al pomo, pomo* meaning a bottle or drink. Very slangy are such words as *piular*, or *gargarear* (gargle).

Bautizar (baptize) means to water down a drink and *con piquete* (sting) is a spiked drink. *Raspabuche* ("scrape-throat") is rot-gut liquor; *aguardiente* (fire water) is moonshine. *Disparar* (to shoot or fire a round) means to spring for the drinks, pick up the tab, buy the round.

A bit of drinking folklore: in Mexico one never orders a last drink—the "one for the road" is *la penúltima* (the next to last) or *la del estribo* (one for the stirrup). It's worth noting, by the way, that in Mexico especially, a *cantina* is a bar for men only. You see Ladies' Bars that admit both sexes.

Beer

Cheve, chevecha, and *chela* are slang for *cerveza* like "suds" or "brewski." One also hears *serpentina* and in the North one hears *birria,* (actually a goat stew) for beer, a joking "Spanishization" of American pronunciation. Omar Onda's favorite T-shirt says *Cheves, Chavas, y Chivas*—Beers, chicks, and the famous Chivas soccer team.

Drunk

Borracho is the common term, directly equivalent, although *ebrio* is more proper and *briago* is heard. *Borrachón* is a drunk, souse, or just somebody who gets drunk a lot. *Emborrachar* means to get drunk. Beto Boca de Basura says, *"Más vale ser un borracho conocido que un Al-*

cohólico Anónimo" (better a well-known drunk than an anonymous alcoholic).

Teporocho also means drunk. *Alumbrado* and *alumbrarse* are, literally, "lit" and "to get lit" and *encandilado* means the same—lit up like a Christmas tree. *Enchispado* (sparky) is a happy drunk and a *cohete* (skyrocket) is a guy who is blasted. You also hear *ahogado* (drowned) and *al color* (stewed) for bombed. Beto gets *bien pedo* (really smashed) every pay day; it's a crude term, since *pedo* means fart.

The Spanish term for "hangover," should you get that far, is one of the most picturesque in the language—*la cruda*. No wonder it eclipses the proper term, *la resaca*. Next time you crude out, try to remember Beto's advice, *"Evite la cruda, permanezca borracho"* (Avoid hangovers, stay drunk). Sober and sobriety, for those interested, are *sobrio* and *la sobriedad* respectively.

Games and Sports

Other than **dominos**, party and bar games generally use dice *(dados)* in games like **cubilete** (with a throwing cup) and **chingona** (with poker dice), or cards (formally **naipes** but **gatas** in the jailhouse and streets).

A deck of cards is a **baraja** and **barajar** is to shuffle the deck. There are different games and even decks in Mexico, but you can find games of spades and poker (cribbage is unknown, alas). Poker terminology is strange, though. Aces are **ases** and kings **reyes** as expected, but queens are **cüinas** and jacks, **jotas** (the letter "j"). Four of a kind is a **poker** and full house is a **ful** (rhymes with "fool"). You play for **fichas** (chips).

You don't find darts in Mexico, but there are **billares** (pool or billiards) and you might find a **boliche** (bowling alley).

When watching sports you will find a proliferation of English terms, even in soccer (which most people know is called **fútbol**). You hear of the **futbolistas** making a **gol**, or being **of-sayd** (offside)—and this is more so in other sports such as *básquetbol*, *box*, *volibol* and *fútbol americano*. One hears of *jonrons* (home runs), *noqueos* (knockouts), and *cachas* (catches). You even hear the ball called *bola*, instead of *pelota*.

There are universal terms like *equipo* (team), *empate* (a tie), *campeonato* (championship), and *temporada* (season), of course. But plays and strategies use a morass of terms that can take years to learn, so it's also usually easier to use English terms for American sports, rather than try to learn complicated Spanish translations like *medio jardinero* (middle gardener) for "center fielder" or *mariscal de campo* (field marshall) for "quarterback."

El que con cojos anda,
se llama bastón.
Atentamente, Muleta

Perro flaco, hasta las
pulgas lo abandonen.

El que tiene miles sufre,
él que debe millones goza.

En pared de clínica de partos:
Por el beso empieza eso.

On the wall of an obstetrics
clinic: Kissing started that.

Una mujer no es la
que vale, es lo que
cuesta.

It's not what a
woman is worth,
it's what she costs.

Siempre quise ser alguien.
Ahora soy yo.

I always wanted to be
someone. Now I'm me.

No lleves a
enterrar a tu
suegra en día
laboral, que
primero está el
deber que el
placer.

Don't bury your
mother-in-law on
a work day.
Business before
pleasure.

No me mires a mí;
mírate tú mismo. —
Espejo

Don't look at me;
look at yourself. —
Mirror

Chapter 8

Nicknames of Origin

Is a *gringo* worse than a *chilango*?

There is a lot of slang directed at geographical origins. This may be innocent or insulting, but don't presume you are being insulted (or insulting) unless there are other grounds beside the use of some hard-to-identify terms. Americans are often politely called *americanos*, but there are those who insist that since "America" is two big continents, Americans should refer to themselves as *norteamericanos* or the unutterable *estadounidenses*. (It should be pointed out that both Canadians and Mexicans are also North Americans and that Mexico is formally "The United States of Mexico.") This makes the familiar term *gringo* seem attractive, but it could be noted that it is a bit of a slur and might embarrass or amuse many Mexicans, like a Black calling himself or allowing himself to be called a "sambo" or "Uncle Tom." A good middle ground is *gabacho*, which is applied almost exclusively to Americans, though it originally meant "Frenchman." The current slang for the French is *franchutes*.

Many Mexican regions have colorful slang terms for their natives, nicknames generally as inexplicable as "Tar heels," "Jay hawkers," and "Knickerbockers." The most common of these is *chilango*, a native of Mexico City or the surrounding Distrito Federal. *Chilangos* use the term proudly, but to others it has varying degrees of deprecation. For instance, there are highway graffiti that say, *"Haz patria, mata a un chilango"* (Be patriotic, kill a Chilango). You hear Mexico City and the D.F. called *Chilangolándia* (and the U.S. called *Gringolándia*.)

Another classic appellation is *tapatío*, a native of Guadalajara. A term of extreme pride and without the negative sentiment of *chilango*, *tapatío* things are very Mexican. *Ojos tapatíos* is a famous song about the distinctive European eyes of *tapatías*, and the real name for the famous "Mexican Hat Dance" is *"Jarabe Tapatío."*

People from Monterrey are called *regiomontanos* and have a reputation for being cheapskates, as Texans have a reputation for being braggarts. In Mexico, by the way, "tightwad" is *codo* (elbow) and can be signified by tapping the elbow.

Other regional nicknames include (but are not limited to):
culiche—from Culiacán, in Sinaloa
hidrocálidos—Aguascalientes
jarochos—Veracruz
jalisquillos—State of Jalisco (a slight slur)
abajeños—The lower (or *abajo*) part of Jalisco
tijuas—Tijuana
choyeros—Ciudad Constitución, B.C.
cachanilla—Baja California, specifically, Mexicali
boxito or *boshito*—the Yucatán peninsula
arascos—Michoacán

campechano—Campeche
alacrán(scorpion)—Durango
jaibo—Tampico
borinqueño—Puerto Rico
gachupín—Spain
chale—China or South East Asia
tejano—Texas (and is the word for a cowboy hat)

El odio le dijo al amor,
< Gracias por amarme tanto. >

Hatred said to Love,
"Thanks for loving me so much."

Cuarentón y solterón, puede que sea maricón.
Atentamente,
La Vecina

Satanás es un pobre diablo.
Atentamente, Jesús

No me empujen,
yo me caigo solo.
Atentamente, El Borracho

Don't push,
I can fall down on my own.
(signed) The Drunk

He oído hablar tan bien de ti que creía que estabas muerto.

I've heard such nice things said of you that I thought you were dead.

Yo fui el primero. El Huevo

I was first. The Egg

El muerto al hoyo y el vivo con la viva.

El presente es un regalo de ayer. Atentamente, Hoy

Chapter 9

Border Slang

Border jargon doesn't just derive from the blending that infuriates purists on both sides; it has it's own wellsprings of new expressions, many from the *barrios* of Tijuana and Los Angeles (or, as the *Pachucos* would say it, "*Los*"). Here's a quick glimpse at this complex web of language.

Cholos are variously L.A. street punks, Mexican American gangsters, or (according to Mexicans) any sort of low rider low-lifes that come south of the border. Though the word is ill-defined, there is a definite *Cholo* style, though it might change. *Cholos* are the cultural descendants of the *Pachucos* (or **Chucos**), who in turn followed the zoot suit Latinos of the 1950's. Much of the border lingo is their invention, although much is also coined by recent immigrants struggling with the language.

The most notable phrase in **Cholo** Spanish is *"Ese"* (that) as an address or referring to someone. Also famous are *"Ahí te huacho"* (I'll "watch" you here—I'll see you later) which is frequently stylized even more to *"Ayte guacho."* The **Cholo caló** is characterized by phrases like *sácala* (take it out) for "spare me some dope," *tirar la vuelta* (throw the corner) for "to die," *nuestro barrio rifa sin zafos* (our neighborhood fights without failing).

Some words are merely slurred Spanish, like *"Quiubo"* from *¿Qué hubo?* to mean "What's with you?" Some are twisted down from English like a customized motorcycle; *biklas* (bikes, motorbikes) for instance, or *chopear* for "chopping" a car, *blofear* for bluffing at poker, or grabbed straight out of English like *los beibidols*.

Others are complex puns and jokes, with syllables added on over the years until they emerge as enigmas like the famous *nariz boleada* (polished nose) to mean simply *nada*. At it's best, the border slang is free-wheeling and spontaneously creative. Along the border there are signs that say, *Se fixean flats* and waitresses who call for *crema de whip*.

A short glossary:

agringarse—to become "gringofied," to adopt Northern ways.

andar lurias—to be crazy, off his rocker

chafa—cheap, low class

echarnos unas birrias—to drink (toss ourselves) some beers

gabardinos—Americans (play on *gabacho*)

jura—cops

grifo—stoned on marijuana

el mono—the movies

buti—*mucho*, a lot

loro—(parrot), friend, *amigo*

pacha—bottle, therefore "booze"

pinero—chatterbox, talkative

pielas—beers

picha—to invite

cofiro—coffee

a pincél—(artist's paintbrush) on foot, walking

tirar bronca—to raise a "beef," to "bitch" at someone

masticar totacha—speak (literally, chew) English

no hay piri—don't worry, no sweat

borlo—a party

cantonear—reside (from *cantón*, house)

de bolón, pin-pon—quickly, chop-chop

tripear por burra—go on a bus trip

clavado—(nailed) in love, having a crush

clavarse—read something or hear it on TV

dompear—to dump

guara—water

raite—a ride, a lift (this is spreading throughout Mexico and is hip among young people in the capital)

bobos—lazy

bonche—bunch

lonche—lunch (in Mexico, one sees *loncherías* and a *lonche* is often a submarine sandwich)

broder—brother

cachar—to catch, or a baseball catcher; catching on in Mexico, since *coger* (to catch) also means to fuck and is therefore awkward to use

chavalo—a kid

checar—to check up

donas—donuts

escuadra—a carpenter's square, therefore a square or nerd
huira—a young girl, chick
hayna—a broad, babe, honey
jale—a job or gig
monis—American money
lisa—(smooth) shirt
pai—pie
pai de queso — cheese cake
piquiniqui—picnic
panqueque—pancakes, or pound cake
saina—a sign, like *saina de neón*

La virginidad mata
... vacúnate.
— Pipí Fantasma

Mi papá vendió la droguería porque no tenía más remedio.
—Sobredosis

Cuando se es como yo ... no se puede ser modesto.

When you are like me ... you can't be modest.

Más poesía ... Menos policía

Cuando me despierto me da hambre, y cuando como me da sueño. ----*Solitario*

When I wake up it makes me hungry, and when I eat it makes me sleepy. ----*Lonely*

Mujer que se hace la estrecha,
con otro se suelta las mechas.
----Colchón

A woman who acts
straight-laced, lets down her
hair with another. ----Mattress

El trabajo es salud ... lo que
mata son los sueldos.

Work is healthy ... what kills is
the salaries.

Si el tabaco le hace mal a tu fuerza
física, deja el deporte.

If tobacco is bad for your physical
strength, leave off sports.

El que
madruga,
sufre de
insomnio.

He who gets
up early,
suffers from
insomnia.

Estudiar es dudar de
las capacidades de tus
compañeros. —
Intelecto

El drama más
emocionante es
la lectura de un
testamento.

To study is to doubt
the capacity of your
companions.
— Intellectual

La inteligencia me persigue ... pero yo soy más veloz.
Intelligence chases after me ... but I'm too fast.

Chapter 10

Some Basics

Greetings

Apart from the often-heard *¿Qué onda?*, *¿Qué transas*? is a hip way to ask what's up or to imply "What's the deal?" (transaction). ***Bien transa***, on the other hand means someone is a cheat. Recently you hear *¿Cómo estamos?* as a greeting. This "How are we doing?" has a friendly ring and is good for the beginner who can't sort out whether to use ***tu*** or ***usted***. A simple ***Buenas*** is handy near midday when you're not sure if it's ***días*** or ***tardes***, and to appear totally cool at any time of the day or night.

Hasta la Bye-bye

Popular ways to say "See you later" are *nos vemos* (we'll see each other) or just *luego* (later), with *al rato* (in a little while) for short-term separations. More formally, one usually hears *Que le vaya bien* (fare you well). *Baybay* (pronounced "bye-bye") is considered hip in Mexico, just as we use "*ciao*," which is also used in Latin America and particularly the heavily Italian Argentina, where it is spelled "*chiau*."

YES, NO, AND WHO

Sí

Yes can be *simón, is, sábanas, cilindros, sifón, cigarros*, and the *pochismo* or "Spanglish" expression, "*Claro que yes*," (a common expression, used in the same spirit that we would say "Who, *moi*?") *Claro* is, of course, the way Spanish speakers say, "Of course," and slangsters often express "sure," "you bet," etc. as *clarón*, or *clarinete*.

Carlos Colegiano ran into Luis Lambada in the street on a hot day and asked his friend if he'd like to join him for a beer. *"¡Simón!"* replied Luis, heavily accenting the second syllable.

No

Nel is popular, especially on the street, and as a sassy response like "Nope" or "Nah," you also hear *Nel pastel*, and *Nones cantones.*

Nada or No Hay

Big concepts in Mexico—*No hay, no hay* is a TV catch phrase seen on bumper stickers and decals (*calcomanías* in Spanish) and often good for a laugh.

Other forms of "no got" are *nadaza, onia, nenél, nanay, ni fu, ni sopa, ni zócalo, ni marta, Negrete, Nicanor, Nicolás*, (and the Spanishized *inglesito* "*never in mai cochin laif*").

Ni jota and other *"ni"* expressions are often used to mean you didn't understand something. Omar Onda asked Olivia if she understood his complicated instructions, "*¿Entien-*

des?" Olivia replied, "*Ni Marta*" (Not a word.) When Beto Boca de Basura asked Berta if she would come over and clean his house she responded, "*Ni sueños*" (Not in your wildest dreams.)

Yo

Even a simple word like "I" gets slanged. Carlos Colegiano says, *Melón, menta, me manta,* or *Yolanda*. Beto Boca de Basura prefers the *caló* gutter slang, *mendurria*.

Tú, Usted

Instead of *tú* or *ti*, slangsters like Luis Lambada often use words like *tunas*, or *tiburcio*. Beto Boca de Basura uses the *caló* expression *mendorasqui* for "you."

Readers may observe here that one can improvise synonyms for *sí, no, yo, mi* and other stock responses by playing with words that start with the same syllable.

FEATURES AND CHARACTERISTICS

The Face

Just as we use words like "mug" and "map," Spanish has slang terms for the face, many stemming from the *caló* term, *fila*. They include: *filharmónica, catequismo, la feroz* (the ferocious), and *fachada* (facade). When Luis Lambada invited Leticia and Berta Boca de Basura for dinner and dancing because he had won at the racetrack, Berta told Leticia, *"Es pura facha"* (He's all front, or all bluff). *"Basta con tu desfachatez,"* (enough of your sass) was Luis's response.

Eyes are sometimes called *candorros, linternas, oclayos* or *ventanas* instead of *ojos* by Carlos Colegiano. In *Caló*, Beto Boca de Basura replaces *ver, mirar* or *observar* (to see, look at) with *mirujear, riflear,* or *clachar.*

The Head

The head is called variously *coco* (coconut), *adobe*, *maceta* (flower pot), *azotea* (a flat roof), *calabaza* (squash, calabash), *chiluca, choya,* and *chayote.*

Feet Get Around

La pata means paw or hoof of an animal, so is used humorously or insultingly. *Meter la pata* means "to put your foot in it" (as in your mouth).

"Did you hear about Beto's father? *Estiró la pata*" (lit. stretched out the foot, means to kick the bucket), Leticia told Olivia Onda.
"*Que mala pata*" (What a bum break), said Olivia, "How did it happen?"
"He fell off the balcony and landed *patas arriba* (upside down) in the rain barrel."

Miscellaneous Terms

achichincle a "brown noser"
alzado snooty, stuck-up
bembo a jerk, a bimbo
berrinche a tantrum
berrinchudo pouting or given to childish fits
bobo an idiot or dunce. Omar Onda always referred to the Mexican soap opera *Cuna de Lobos* (Cradle of Wolves) as *Cuna de Bobos.*
bruto coarse, uncouth, redneck
bicho a bug or any tiny animal, an insignificant person, used chidingly

like twerp or knucklehead
burra, veloz bicycle
bola a street brawl, a "rumble"
cabula pesado, a jerk or creep (adjective or noun)
camellar (literally, to "camel") to walk or stroll; at the border it means to work, especially in the field
carterista a pickpocket
chabacano cheap, vulgar, common, low class
chévere cool, hip, especially in Central America
chiflado crazy, loony, *loco*
chinche (bedbug) a pest, obnoxious person
piropo compliment, but to give lavish compliments to the opposite sex is *echar flores* (throw flowers)
paparrucha a fib or white lie
conchudo (having a shell) a cynic, a "hard case"
corriente cheap, vulgar, common (said of people, or language)
cucaracha a jalopy or "beater," also *carrucha, carcacha*
dar color (to give color) street talk for knowing or recognizing someone
No te doy color is "I don't know you from Adam."
dengue prude, sissy, prissy
espantajo (scarecrow) weirdo, freak
feón an ugly sucker

media feona is "about half ugly"

güero refers to light hair or skin, thus can mean "fair," "Whitey," "Blondie." In Mexico often used as a synonym for gringo.

cantón house, is common street talk, but widely understood; also *cantera, cuartel, chantel* or *jaula* (cage); *gan* or *chachimba* are gutter slang.

changuita (little monkey) your "squeeze," the girl you are making it with at the moment

fusca a pistol

grueso a punk, "greaseball," street scum, biker

jalonero or *jaladar* good company, a cool person to hang out with

¡lagarto! (lizard) is a cry to take away bad luck

lagartitos are pushups

lata (tin can) a hassle, bother, pain in the butt

lépero (leper) a foul-mouthed, obscene creep, a "gross-out artist"

ligue (from *ligar*, to tie up) means a sexual or romantic conquest (or *conquista*, as they say)

lucha libre wrestling, especially professional style

llanta (tire) "spare tire" of fat, love handles, midriff bulge

mamón or *mamey* a jerk, a pain in the ass

mandilón (from *mandil*—apron) hen-pecked or "apron-stringed"
muy gente (literally, very people) salt of the earth, jolly good fellow
naco nerd or hick, low-class oaf

palanca (lever) pull, clout. Luis asks Beto why he tries to be friends with Carlos Colegiano. *"Carlos tiene palanca con el ayuntamiento"* (He's got pull at City Hall), Beto replies.

pissed off—*enojado* can be "slangized" to *encabronado*, or phrases like *Me choca* or *Me crispa*
chocante is obnoxious, a piss-off
pichón (pigeon) a sucker, a chump, or a mark
gusano (worm) the railroad
ranfla (used only in the border area) slang for a custom rod or low rider car, "wheels"
¡saco! said when breaking wind
li is common for *calle*, street; also *calletana, lleca,* and *fiusa*
tianguis swap meet, flea market
tijera (scissors) a tattle tale, a fink
tilico starved, a walking skeleton
tocayo namesake, person (or saint) with same name
trompillo "the raspberry," farting sound made with the lips

quedada (one left or ignored) a wall-flower
zafado crazy, *loco*
zonzo a moron, a gooner

El borracho se
acuesta con mujeres
hermosas y se
despierta con feas.

The drunk goes to
bed with beautiful
women and wakes
up with ugly ones.

Lo único que los
nudistas no dejan
ver es la ropa.

The only thing that
nudists don't show
off is clothing.

Del árbol caído, todos hacen su asiento.

Mi mamá no me permite tener novia.
—Edipo

My mother won't let me have a
girlfriend. —Oedipus

Las mujeres de senos pequeños son inteligentes, pero a mi me gustan bien brutas.

Si todo el mundo escribiera lo que piensa ya sabriamos la verdad de la vida.

Si su amorcito llora, dele Coca Cola.
Si sigue llorando, dele por la cola.
Atte. Chispa de la vida

Soy viejo
pero subo
y bajo.
Atentamente,
el peso

$

Cristo viene.
Unica presentación
Madison Scuar Garden

Antes de conocerte tenía malos pensamientos, ahora que estoy contigo los disfruto

Cuando cague piense, para que
cuando piense no la cague

¿Para qué fingir cariño
si ya hicimos el amor?

Esta vida es un charco de mierda
que hay que cruzar nadando ... pero
si no se sabe nadar hay que cruzar
tragando.

Bellas ellas entre las bellas,
pero más bellos ellos entre las
ellos de ellas.

Al mal amante
le estorban hasta
las tetas

No dejes para mañana la suegra que
puedas matar hoy.
——Pasado Mañana

Índice Español

English Index

order form

Publications from *Bueno* Books:

____ Spanish Lingo for the Savvy Gringo $14.95
____ Bilingual Cooking: *La Cocina Bilingüe* $5.00
____ Native Speaker:
.Teach English & See the World $5.00
____ Mexican Slang plus Graffiti $9.95

Mark quantity of each book you want.
Please add local sales tax and $3 postage for the entire order. We'll also send you our complete catalog including our latest titles and a sample of ***Bueno***, the newsletter of *friendly foreign language learning™*. Please send book(s) to:

name_____

address_____

city, state, zip_____

Mail your order to:

Bueno Books
PO Box 847
Round Rock TX 78680-0847

Credit card orders, call **1-800-356-9315**
Bookstores, call 1-800-626-6579